How do I use t

Key Words with Peter a
parallel series, each contain
series are written using the sa
vocabulary. Readers will get the most out of **Key Words** with
Peter and Jane when they follow the books in the pattern
1a, 1b, 1c; 2a, 2b, 2c and so on.

• Series a
gradually introduces and repeats new words.

• Series b
provides further practice of these same words, but
in a different context and with different illustrations.

• Series c
uses familiar words to teach **phonics** in a methodical way,
enabling children to read increasingly difficult words.
It also provides a link to writing.

Published by Ladybird Books Ltd
A Penguin Company
Penguin Books Ltd., 80 Strand, London WC2R 0RL, UK
Penguin Books Australia Ltd, 707 Collins Street, Melbourne, Victoria 3008, Australia
Penguin Group (NZ) 67 Apollo Drive, Rosedale, North Shore 0632, New Zealand

019

ISBN: 978-1-40930-126-4

Printed in China

Key Words

with Peter and Jane

7a

Happy holiday

written by W. Murray
illustrated by J.H. Wingfield

Peter and Jane are going to have a holiday away from home. They are going to the house of their aunty and uncle, who live by the sea. Aunty is their mother's sister.

Mother is going to take them to her sister's house, but she is not going to be with the children on their holiday. She has to be at home to look after Father.

The two children like their aunty and uncle very much. They have been to their house before, and now they talk about the good times they have had on holidays there.

Their aunty and uncle have no children of their own, but they love children and like to be with them. They like to talk to them, to play with them, and to take them out.

They are off now, and
are going fast along the road.

"I like to go fast when it is a good road,"
says Peter.

"Yes," says Jane. "I like to go fast, but
not too fast."

"It is a good road," says Mother, "and
the man will not go too fast."

The sun is out, but the day is not too
hot. They look out of the windows. They
can see the hills and the trees as they go
by.

"I love to see the flowers and the trees," says Jane.

"Your uncle is on holiday too," says Mother, "so he will take you where you want to go."

"Good," says Peter. "He will come into the sea with us. I know he likes the water."

"Aunty likes the water too," says Jane, "so she will come. It will be fun. It will be a good holiday for us."

The children are at the house of their aunty and uncle.

"How nice to see you all, my dears," says Aunty.

"Do come in," says Uncle. "You must want your tea. Let me take your things."

"Yes, it is nice to see you again," says Mother, "and we do want some tea." The two sisters sit down to talk as they have their tea. The children go into the garden with their uncle to see his dog.

"What a dear little dog!" says Jane.

"Yes, he is nice," says Peter. "Will you let us take him for a walk?" he asks.

"Yes," says his uncle, "but come and have your tea now."

The children have tea and then go to see their mother off. "Be good children," she says, "and have a nice holiday."

"Yes, Mum," they say. "We will see you again soon."

The next day Uncle says to the two children, "I am going to take the dog for a walk. Do you want to come?"

"Yes, please," says Peter. "We want to see the sea."

They go on a road where they can look down at the sea.

"I am not going to walk too fast," says Uncle. "Then you can look over at the sea and the boats."

"It is nice up here," says Peter. "I like to see the boats on the water. Look at that red one over there. I want to go into the water this afternoon."

"It is going to be very hot this afternoon," says Uncle, "so it will be nice to go into the sea. We must go home now as it is one o'clock."

Jane looks after the dog. "You are a dear little dog," she says. "Will you come into the water with us? Come on home now, it is time to eat."

It is about three o'clock in the afternoon and they are all on the sands down by the sea. Aunty sits on the sands with Jane and the dog, and Peter is in the water with Uncle.

"Are you too hot, dear?" Aunty asks Jane.

"No, I am not too hot. It is nice to be in the sun," says Jane. "I can go into the water if I get too hot."

Peter calls the dog, and it runs fast over the sands into the water.

"Look at the dog," says Aunty. "He loves it down here with us."

Peter calls Jane and Aunty. "Come into the water with us," he says, "and bring the ball with you, please."

They go into the water and take the ball to play with the others.

After some time they all come out of the water onto the sands to have some tea.

The children like to be on the sands in the sun. "It is fun here," says Peter. "I always want to run and jump when I am on the sands."

Aunty calls to him, "Bring the dog from the water and come and have tea." Then she says, "Sit down here with me, dear, and don't eat too fast."

They all have tea, and then Peter asks Jane to walk on the sands with him by the water. "Why?" asks Jane.

"We will see what we can find," Peter says. "We will be back soon," he calls to his uncle.

Off they go. As they walk they look at the sands and the water. "The sea brings things in," says Peter. "There is always something to find."

Soon they hear Aunty call them back. "Why does she call?" asks Peter.

"It is time to go now," says Aunty. "Come on, you two."

It is another day. This afternoon the children are on the sands again.

"Uncle gave me some money," says Peter.

"I have some money too," says Jane. "What are we going to do?"

"Let us go and look at the donkeys," says Peter. "We always do that on our holiday."

The brother and sister walk over the sands to the donkeys. There are big ones and little ones, and a man and a boy with them.

Peter and Jane look at the children as they go up and down on the donkeys.

"Do you want to have a go?" asks Jane.

"Yes," Peter says, "why not? I am going on a big one. Come on, Jane, you have one, too."

Jane calls the man who brings up a donkey. He helps Jane up on its back. The boy brings up another one, and Peter gets on it.

The two children are on the donkeys' backs. The man takes the money from Peter first and then from Jane. "Don't go along the road," he says. "Please keep on the sands."

Off they go over the sands. Peter is first, and then comes Jane. She calls out to Peter, "We must not go too fast.'

"I know," says Peter. "You come after me."

His donkey walks along the sand by the water. Jane's comes after it.

Then Peter stops. "Why do you stop?" asks Jane.

"I don't know why," says Peter. "Come on," he says to his donkey. "Don't stop, please. Come along." Then he pats it and off they go again.

After some time they come back to the donkey man. "Thank you," says Peter, as they get off.

Jane says to her donkey, "Thank you, you are a dear little donkey. We will come back another day."

"It is four o'clock," says Jane. "It is not time to go back home, so we can see some more. First let us go over there with all the children. Come along, Peter, come along. Let us see Punch and Judy. We always see Punch and Judy on every holiday."

"Yes," says Peter, "it is nice to see Punch and Judy at any time."

The brother and sister go with all the other children to look at Punch and Judy. There are big boys and girls, and little ones. A father and mother bring their baby to see. They all have fun.

"I like this," says Jane. "We must come to see Punch and Judy another day. They are always here in the afternoon."

A man comes round with a hat for some money. "Have you any money?" Jane asks Peter. "Put some in the hat as he comes by us."

"I like to see Punch and Judy," says Jane, as they walk away. "I wish we could see them every day."

"Yes," says Peter, "I wish we could have Punch and Judy at home. We could see them any day then."

As they walk over the sands they look at the pier. "I wish we could go on the pier," says Peter. "It is fun on the pier."

"We have time, and I have some money," says Jane, "so why not go on the pier now?"

"Good," says Peter. "Come along then."

First the children give the man their money and then they walk along the pier. They look down into the sea, and at the boats on it.

"Let us see if the men have any fish,"
says Peter. They talk to the men as they
fish.

They look back at the sands. "I can see
the donkeys, and the Punch and Judy,"
says Peter.

Peter and Jane are at the end
of the pier. There is a motor boat at
the end of the pier and Peter and Jane
can look down into the motor boat.

"It would be nice if we could go out in
the motor boat. I wish we could," says
Peter. "Have you any money, Jane?"

"No," says Jane, "I have no money,
and it is time to go back home for tea."

"We could always come back another
day," says Peter. "If we go out in the motor
boat, Aunty and Uncle will want to come."

"Yes, they would want to be with us,"
says Jane. "We must ask them first."

They see the motor boat go off from the end of the pier. It is very fast.

"Come on," says Jane. "We must go home for tea now. We will come on the pier again this holiday."

The next morning Peter tells his aunty and uncle about the motor boat at the end of the pier. He asks his uncle if he will take them out in it.

"Yes," says Uncle. "I would like to go. We could go this morning if you wish."

"I could come this morning, and I would like to go," says Aunty. "But I don't want to get wet."

"No," says Peter, "you will not get wet because it is a big motor boat."

"May we bring the dog?" asks Aunty.

"Yes, we may," says Peter. "I saw a dog in the motor boat when we were on the pier."

"Yes," says Jane, "we saw one when we were there." She pats the dog. "You can come along with us in the motor boat," she says. "You are always a good dog."

"The boat will not go too fast, Aunty," says Peter. "You will like it."

"One, two, three, four," says Peter. "There are four of us. We will want four seats in the motor boat."

"Yes," says Jane, "we will want four seats, but there are five of us, with the dog. One, two, three, four, five."

All five get into the big motor boat at the end of the pier. It is a hot morning.

"May we have seats at the back, please?" Uncle asks the man, as he comes for the money.

"Yes, we would like to sit at the back, please," says Aunty.

The man takes their money and they all sit down. Jane has a seat by Aunty and Peter's seat is by Uncle. All four look happy, and the dog looks happy, too.

Off they go. Soon the motor boat is going very fast.

"This is nice," calls out Peter to Jane.

"Yes," calls out Jane, "I like to fly along like this."

They all get out of the motor boat at the end of the pier. Jane looks happy and Peter looks happy, too. "I think that was the best morning of the holiday," he says. "I like going fast like that. I wish we could do that every day."

"We were going much too fast for me," says Aunty. "I would like some tea."

"I think there is a café on the pier," says Uncle. "We could go in there."

They find the café, and all five go in. Uncle asks Peter and Jane what they would like.

"I think I would like an ice-cream, please," says Peter.

"An ice-cream for me too, please," says Jane.

"May we have tea for two and two ice-creams, please?" Uncle asks the girl in the café.

Soon the girl brings the tea and the ice-creams. From their seats in the café they look out over the sea.

The children look at the rain on the windows and Peter says,

"Rain, rain, go away,
Come again another day,"
but the rain does not stop.

"I will write some letters," says Jane.

"Yes, I will write some letters, too," says Peter. "Aunty will help us."

"I will write to Mum and Dad. You write to Grandmother and Grandfather," says Jane.

Peter says, "We will write letters to our friends Pam, Mary, Bob and Molly, and Mr and Mrs Green."

Aunty helps the children with their letters. In her letters Jane tells about her happy holiday, about the donkeys, Punch and Judy, and the ice-cream in the café. In his letters Peter writes about the dog, the pier, and the morning in the motor boat.

"It is five o'clock," says Aunty. "You were good to write the letters. Now we will have tea."

"Here is a letter from Mum," calls out Jane. "Help me read it, Peter."

"Yes," says Peter, "I hope we can read it."

Aunty comes in. "May I help you?" she asks.

This is what they read—
Dear Jane and Peter,

It is time to write you a letter. First of all I hope you are well, and that Aunty and Uncle are well, too. We are all well here. Dad sends his love.

We hope you have a happy holiday, and that it does not rain. Be good children, and don't eat too much ice-cream.

Mrs Green gave me some eggs this morning. It was nice of her. The children send you their love.

I saw your teacher today. She hopes you have a good time.

The cat and the dog are well.

I think I must stop now, as it is five o'clock. I will write again soon.

All my love,
Mum.

Every day the ice-cream van comes down the road where Aunty and Uncle live. All the girls and boys in the road like to see the ice-cream van.

When it is hot many children come out to buy ice-creams from the man in the van, but if it rains not many of them come out to buy.

This morning, there is no rain and the sun is out. Jane and Peter hope that Aunty will send them out to buy ice-creams.

"Here he comes!" calls Peter. "I can see him at the end of the road! Tell Aunty, Jane. Where is she?"

"I think she was going to write some letters," says Jane. "I will go and tell her that the van is here."

Jane comes back with Aunty. Aunty gives the children some money and sends them out to buy ice-creams. Many children are at the van today.

It is hot again today.

Peter is in the water with his new boat in his hand. The water is blue, and Peter's boat is blue and red.

"It was good of Uncle to buy you a new boat," says Jane. She has a doll in her hands.

"Yes," says Peter, "and it was nice of Aunty to let you have her old doll. I hope you like it."

"Yes, I do," says Jane. "Aunty had this doll when she was a little girl."

Peter puts his blue and red boat into the water, and pulls it round with his hand. "It is going well," he says.

Many children are in the water. Peter finds a friend who lives next door to his aunty and uncle.

This boy is Tom, and he has a motor boat which he hands to Peter. "It is new," he says. "My Dad gave it to me." Tom's motor boat is blue and green.

Uncle found out that the children had never had a kite.

"So you have never had a kite," he said. "All boys and girls must know how to fly a kite. I must send you to buy a new one. Here is some money. Go to the toy shop by the café."

The children have found the toy shop. First they look in the window. They can see many toys. There are motor boats and cars, dolls and a Punch and Judy, and an ice-cream van. But they do not see any kites.

"Let us go in," says Jane. "I think the man in the shop may help us."

"Yes," says Peter, "I hope so."

"Kites?" says the man in the shop. "There were some here. Yes, here they are." He hands them a blue one, and a red one.

"Do you want the blue or the red?" he asks.

"The red one, please," says Peter.

"Did you get your kite?" asks Aunty.

"Yes, we did, we found just what we wanted," says Jane. "We are just going to fly it." She calls the dog.

The children go off up the hill to fly their new kite. "Here we are at the top," says Peter. "This should be just what we want."

Peter runs fast with the kite. The dog runs after him. He wants to get the kite.

Peter stops. "Why did you bring the dog, Jane?" he asks. "He should never have the kite."

"No," says Jane, "he should never have the kite." She says to the dog, "Come here. You must never have it."

"Should we send him home?" asks Peter.

"No," says Jane. "I will keep him by me when you run."

Peter runs off again. He pulls the kite along after him, but it does not go up.

They have never had a kite. They do not know how to fly their new kite at first. "It should go up but it will not go," Peter tells Jane. "I don't know the right way to fly it."

"Just let me have a go," says Jane. She runs along fast with the kite, but it does not go up.

"That's what I did," says Peter. "That's not the right way."

A woman comes along. She is a nice woman, out for a walk with her dog.

"Let me tell you the right way," the woman says. "This is what I did when I was a little girl."

She tells Peter he should take up the kite in his hands, then she tells Jane she should run fast and pull.

The kite is going up and up.

"We have found the right way," calls Peter, as he runs. "Look at it going up now."

The children tell Uncle and Aunty that they had a good time with the new kite. They talk about the nice woman who gave them help.

"Would you like to go out to the woods for a picnic?" asks Aunty.

"I love the woods," says Peter. "Yes, let us have a picnic tea in the woods."

"Yes," says Jane, "it is just what I should like."

"We have found a nice place in the woods for a picnic," says Aunty. "You have never been there before, but I think you will like it. It is a good way to go, so we will have to take the car."

"It is the right day for a picnic, as it is so hot," says Uncle. "I am going to get the car now."

Soon they are in the woods.

"It is a nice place," says Jane.

"Yes," says Peter, "a nice place for a picnic, and a nice place to play."

On their way to the shops the children talk about the picnic in the woods. They talk about going home to Mum and Dad.

They are going to buy a present for Mum and a present for Dad.

"I want a good look round," says Jane. "I don't know what to get for my present."

"Do you think they would like a picture?" asks Peter. "I think I will get a picture for my present."

"Yes," says Jane, "give them a picture about our holiday. They would like that."

The children look round the shops for their presents. Peter soon finds a picture he likes. It is of the sea and the sands.

Jane buys a book for her present. It is a book about flowers. The woman in the shop tells her all about the book.

When they get back Aunty and Uncle see the presents and say how nice they are.

This morning Mother came to take the children back to their own home, on the bus. Aunty and Uncle saw them off.

Peter has their new kite and his blue and red boat. Jane has her doll and the presents. She tells Mother about the presents.

"The picture is from Peter," she says. "It is a picture of the sea and the sands. The book is from me. It is a book about flowers. You should like it. The woman in the shop said you would."

"Yes," says Mother, "Dad and I will like the picture and the book very much. We will always keep them. Thank you very much."

Peter looks out of the window. "This is the way," he says. "This is the right road. I can see the place in the wood where we had our picnic. We did have fun there. We had fun every day. It was a happy holiday."

New words used in this book

Total number of new words: 67
Average repetition per word: 12